Until I Write

Poems Found at Dawn

Cosimo DeFrancesco

The Awakened Press
www.theawakenedpress.com

For information about special discounts for bulk purchases, please contact The Awakened Press at books@theawakenedpress.com.

The Awakened Press can bring authors to your live event. For more information or to book an event contact books@theawakenedpress.com or visit our website at www.theawakenedpress.com.

Cover and book design by Kurt A. Dierking II

Printed in Canada and the United States of America
First The Awakened Press trade paperback edition

ISBN: 979-8-9860377-7-6

Until
I
Write

Poems Found at Dawn

Cosimo DeFrancesco

The Awakened Press

I have wondered what life would be like without you by my side.

It is hard to picture a world that is no longer perfect.

Contents

Steady

Resilience

About the Author

Love

Naked

I want to be able to stand in front of you
In a way I have never done before
In a way you will remember
In a way I can never forget

I want to be naked
But fully clothed
Naked in emotion
Naked in our trust
Extending the bonds between our fingertips
So they can link like chains
Even across endless fields
So we can always stay connected

I want to be naked
With every aspect of my being
Standing on end
As I feel your current
Coursing through me

Keep me embedded in your thoughts
Let me walk your mind as a guest
So I can search like no one has done before
The ways that make you happy
The ways that make you sad
The ways that make you

Lock yourself in a cage alone
Just so I can find the key
Trapped underneath your terror
To unlock your strength
Let free your joy
Bringing light to your darkness forever

I stand here
Naked
Upon the edge of your thoughts
Hoping you will pull me back in
Even when falling back
Seems to be the easiest way to go
Plummeting off the Earth
Drifting into space
Like a star
Ready to supernova

I stand here naked
I stand here waiting
For you

Moment of Time

Sorry to interrupt you
I would like to take a moment of your time
It won't take long
There are just a few things I need to say

I write to you with no boundaries in mind
No limit to my expression
No restriction to my actions

I remember
When I first set my eyes upon you
That moment of time
The immediate uncontrollable urge
To fall for you
When I never said a word to you
Though if I can formulate thoughts
And words
Of how it must feel to be with you
Maybe
Just maybe
The real thing will be the same
I know
The real thing is better
Our moment in time is now
It passes by each day
As a continuum
Constantly moving
As we grow and move within this world
Our moment of time
When my hand
Releases its pressure from the pen it is holding
And the weight pressing down on the page
Of which these words are being written

Now
The distance between my pen
And this page
Seems more distant
Than the edges of the universe
Where all we see are the stars
That my pen connects
Like a river between oceans
It bends and flows
As each character is formed
Mended onto the page
Creating words
Phrases
And verses
Until another poem of you is written

A Letter to You

You probably have no idea
Why on Earth are you reading this letter?
Why not an email
Or a text message

Why would someone take the time to write out on paper
A message that can simply be received instantly?

The answer is quite simple
I think you can figure it out
Though if you seem to be struggling
Pondering the various scenarios
In which a letter
So plain
Yet so bold
Subtle
Yet so daring
Will be written for you
I can help you with your problem

When one writes a letter
Every word is carefully chosen
Every thought is drawn out of the mind
Extracting only the parts worth mentioning
To make sure
Your time was not wasted
Because these words
Are formed in a way
From someone
Who truly cares about the reaction to them
Inserting punctuation
In locations
Where you should think about what was written
Even if you need to read the line over again
Even if you need to read the line over again
That is likely why it was written

To never be forgotten
To always be stuck inside your mind

I've wanted to get this to you sooner
I wanted to write faster than my heart can beat
But the problem was
Every time I thought of you
My heart skipped
And my hand fell behind
From every word added to this letter
And after completing this letter
An overwhelming feeling will occur

This emotion
Is unpredictable
Unexpected
Unbearable
An emotion
You cannot even describe
While it takes over your senses
Leaving you motionless
Sitting within your living room
Glancing upward to view the street
As a little boy on his bike
Rides by your window
And you realize
Looking into the past
Everything that has culminated
Until now
Here
With you and me

This is where this letter ends
Nothing else to be written
Or said
Because every new word
Breaks further the fabric
That holds this paper together
And with what remains
Enough room
For a signature

Sincerely yours,

A Flower

I am a flower
Blossoming during the summertime
Growing to be as tall as a tower
Not knowing the distance of the climb

To grow as if nothing will stop me
Like floating on air
The higher I go the more I am free
There is nothing that can compare

Yet this time I am restricted
Something is holding me back
My roots have never been so constricted
It seems my heart is where I lack

Today I am near the ground
Wondering what will happen
I can hear every sound
Feeling the earth around me

Why have I not grown?
I can feel the sun's rays
When I grew you were known
Your sight is where I gaze

Until now I never knew
That you are the one I needed
With your love I grew
And have always succeeded

Theatre

I wish to take you
To a place where at night
The people are just as awake
As they are during the day

I wish to take you
Where lights shine over the sky
Cast up from oversized flashlights
Marking its entrance

I wish to walk you
Through the central grand doors
Decorated with floral and geometric patterns
Outlining its limits of restriction
While we make our way through them

As we make our way through the foyer
Lights shining down on us
As the sound of jazz music fills the air
Bouncing off of the Victorian-style architecture
Making ripples in the pool under the large water fountain
That is placed in the centre of the room

I wish to take you
Walk you up and down
Every aisle and every row
Move over
All of the cushioned chairs
Just to find the best view

I wish to sit you
Under the terrace
With no obstruction
Just to keep you in sight

And when the show is over
I wish to take you upon the stage
Right to the centre
With the spotlight on you
Staring out into an audience of one

If Only This Poem Was Written

If only I can put into words
And write a poem of how I feel at this very moment
Or any moment
When I think of you
If only,
As I walk around a corner
Just once
To see you standing there
As I have hoped for
If only,
When I look up into the sky
I smell your scent in the air
Or when I look into the distance
I see your silhouette along the ground
I may be able to write this poem
If only I was with you more
Able to memorize
The way you look at me
The way you look at others
The way you smile
The way you laugh
The way you cry
The way you speak
The way you treat others
I can only do so much to write a poem
If only,
I can turn these words into time
I would never stop writing
Just to keep you near forever
If only,
These words can close the distance
This poem would only be one word:
"Us"
If only,
Any other circumstance of which we can be together
This poem would be written
But this poem can never be written

Journey through My Mind

My mind wanders and searches for you
I know it can't last long
Many doors, but only one is true
To find the one where I belong

As I look around, I see the areas of my mind
None are of the same kind
From the dark to light, happy to sad
To the deepest pits running mad

While walking I hear a tune
There, one door has remained
If this is not it, I shall go insane
Because I would love to see you soon

When I reach the door, I begin to shake
This can't be an earthquake
And as I hear the beat of my heart
Forever pounding from the start

Grabbing the door and pulling it open
I see you and I am amazed
My wondrous journey was just the token
When I saw your eyes, I couldn't help but gaze

As we left the depths of my mind
I knew I would never be back
And towards the end we suddenly sat
Just remembering that she was my greatest find

For when we finally exited my mind
Both of our hearts were truly aligned

As One

As I look across you're all I see
  When I first saw you it hit me
Without you I can never be free
  You were the one that is meant to be

Every time I see you smile
  Glancing over to see you stare
I've wanted to know you for a while
  Getting to know you was only fair

Looking at what we do as one
  Growing closer as time went by
From everything we have won
  Always knowing that we gave this a try

For as one everything is as it should
We seem to know we always could

This Is for You

I've wanted to tell you how I feel about you
But never knew where to start
And in my mind
It usually went something like this:
"I think you are awesome,"
But you see
There is so much more to that than what you might think

When I say you are awesome
I am not only describing the physical
But the mental
The way you formulate words
And phrases
That wrap around my body
As if I am tied
Encircled
By your ability
To make me feel alive

When I say you are awesome
I am telling you
That when you smile
It is like fireflies dancing in the moonlight
Illuminating the area around them
That when you smile
I feel the sun's rays grace my skin
As if staring directly into it
That when you smile
Everything is right in the world
Even when it is not
Because your smile
Gives me hope
For each day to come
For every step I take
Moving forward
Though always looking back

And even if you are not there
Your smile will shine
Breaking the fabric of air
Just as though a hand
Pulling my heart from my chest
Placing it between you and I
In order for your smile
To heal wounds
That never truly mended

Not only your smile
But your mind
Moulds images inside my head
Forming the words
That you are reading
Sometimes it takes a while for me
To take something so beautiful
And turn it into words
I do not think it can even be done
Because words are just lines organized in a way
Forming letters
Making constructs of meanings
In order to understand
What our eyes have been blessed with

Even if these words don't capture the beauty
I truly admire
A quick step
In front of a mirror
Will remind you of true beauty
Regardless of what makeup
Or clothes you are wearing
Because true beauty
Lies deeper than the fabric of your skin
And when I see you
I am in awe
Because all I see is perfection

I know I have not said everything
You just have to understand
There is only so much I can write
Until my hands begin to tremble
The pen becoming too heavy to lift
Reminding myself
Words can only say so much
And in the upcoming silence
You are hearing the most

Struggle

I am trying to find a way
To bring you back to where we were
The warm summer day
When we became lost amongst street signs
Oblivious to the destination we knew nothing about

I am searching for
The moment I can fall into
A time where nothing else matters anymore
Only me and only you
Struggling to let go of one another

I continue to pace around my room
Concluding that I have made no progress since I have started
My mind winning a battle my body never knew began
I am drowning in my own disappointment

I am lost
From waves crashing upon a shore that I have built with my own hands
Sand carried from the place we met
Only to be washed away by waters I am too afraid to jump in

I am loved
Not knowing how to reciprocate
Without destroying myself and others around me
As if I were a tsunami
Engulfing any chance of happiness

I see you every day
I feel your presence
I picture us forever
I want you to know

I am struggling

I am hurting
For no reason but the constant thoughts in my head telling me to suffer

I am ready for you
I will continue to work every day
But on those setbacks
I need you to know
You are the only reason for returning
Be patient
I hope I do not disappoint you

Sadness

Pocket Watch

Keep me near
Hold me close
Never let this time slip so easily by
Like the air that passes through your hair
Or the sand
That you grasp with each hand
Watch
As it trickles through your fingers

Let me open up
When the time is right
So I know that every second
Spent together
Means more than the definition of time
Because with every look into your eyes
Time stops
Even for a second
I stand in awe
Of who is in front of me

Have me by your side
Handle me with care
Like the pocket watch you once owned
Before it fell for you
Shattering into a thousand pieces
Unable to be put back together

I will keep reminding you
Of the time we are in
The moments we are sharing together
I'll be your pocket watch
But unlike your last
When I fall and hit the ground
I will not break

Knowing Is Half the Battle

Every avenue of my thought
Corroded with sidewalks and speed bumps
Occupying space my mind cannot control
Expanding in areas I thought were not possible

I want to ask
Even if I don't want to know the answer
The detrimental thoughts it will leave me with
How can I fix this?
How will I know?
When my mind is clear
Like the sky without a cloud placed in it
Or an ocean without life to explore it

What reason will I come up with?
What excuses will I make?
In order for a pleasant ending
For the terror that arises at night
Ends with the brightest of sunrises
While every rainfall in spring dries
Leaving endless fields of foliage
Illuminating the area around them
With the colour of their leaf

As I look up to the sky
The wind rushing across the landscape
Erupting like dust in a sandstorm
Blinding my sight
Making me unable to see my feet
With every stride further
I begin to sink
Within the earth
Like quicksand I depress into the land
Drowning headfirst underneath my troubles

When I try to make a sound
My vocal cords squeeze
As if being strangled by a python
I struggle for breath
I struggle for my life

Only through this
I am able to ask
Reaching deeper than the question presented
Gathering an answer that does not need understanding
Just acceptance
Knowing the moment when it is my end

Worried

Worried
Failing to wake up in the morning
Forgetting my water bottle at home
Not getting to my destination on time
Losing love
Losing the woman I hope to spend the rest of my life with

Crashing my car
Breaking a bone
My daughter growing older
Finding ways to spend less time with her dad

Falling asleep too late
Or too early
Not getting enough sleep because of it
Losing a friend
Losing a family member
Losing my mind
My sense of self

One day looking into a mirror
Only to stare into the eyes of a stranger
Unable to be altered
Someone I cannot recognize
Someone who I dislike
Trapping me in this state
Not knowing if breaking the glass
Will shatter the remaining parts
That are keeping the rest of myself together

I am worried
That everything I have done
Everything I am doing
Makes no difference

Bathe

Help me find my way back
When getting lost among familiar streets
Was our way of escaping reality

Back when
There was nothing to worry about
Only our happiness

Back when
We did not know what tomorrow held
But what today had

It only felt like yesterday we could not contain our voices
Echoing across empty streets
Lighting the path to our next destination

That light brought us together
Just to soak in the moments
And bathe in its delight

Help me find my way back
So I can bring it to today
And into the future
Somehow what I had got lost along the way
I am still trying to get it back

A Love Letter to Loneliness

Thank you for always being there for me
You always found a way to get back into my life
Even when I was not prepared for you

When looking for advice
You never hesitate to share your thoughts
Letting me know that it is okay to take a step back
From a world revolving around like a spin top slowing in its rotation

I am learning that
No one can replace you
You are the comfy spot on the couch
I could go sit on the other pillows
But I always end up lying down
With my head resting against you

When I am with you
I feel safe
No one can harm me
You keep them from getting close
Like barbed wire
Anyone who tries to get near
Only gets hurt on their way through

When I look at you
I know
You aren't going anywhere
Even when others are trying to pull me away from you

I am worried
What will happen when that day comes
The day when I find out I no longer need you
Will you put up a fight?
Will you let me go?

Please let me go

For Now

I can't find the words anymore
Along this endless maze I've been walking
This maze of words that I cannot describe
What is going on within my mind

I have been here before
Ever so recognizable
Like the sound a wave makes
As it hits the edge of the ocean

While here
Everything is still
Every path seems to go on forever
A maze that has no exit

There are only extra paths
Meant to distract
Delay the search for the exit
The destination which seems invisible.

Only when looking up
Sun beating against my face
Rejuvenating the senses
Restoring my mind.

Then a gust of wind rushing across this path
Hitting my back as if forcing me forward
Then my eyes focus on the spot
That has not been present

This spot was the exit
My escape
Toward a new journey
Toward happiness

Past Memories Make Great Stories

I am proud of myself
Of all my successes
And my faults
I am proud
Of every scar
And every tear shed
I am proud of where they came from
I am proud
Of every heartache
Every pleasure
Every joy
And every pain

Every time I walk
I feel the soreness of yesterday
With every stone my feet touch
While stepping into tomorrow
I feel the wind of the present
As it sails into the past and back
As the current changes around me

While I look into the distance
Staring into the stars
Trying to point out each one
Trying
As if I am searching
Through years of thoughts
When I became me
And everyone else
Became stars

With every inch of each step
Memories appear
As if it is happening right in front of me
Remembering why I am here

Forgotten

Am I beginning to lose myself?
As time passes
My mirror no longer reflects my present
It only portrays who I was before I stopped dreaming

I remember a time
When every day was a new adventure
There was always something new to look forward to
Now
It seems
There are fewer days for adventure
Fewer moments that I look forward to

What else can I do
When a routine is no longer a routine
But a shackle
Preventing any new experience
Each day blending into another
Each day
Repeating
Wake, work, eat, sleep
Wake, work, eat, sleep
Wake... work... eat... sleep
Wake... work... eat... sleep

I have had a rule
To never say goodbye

In my eyes
Saying goodbye is permanent
There is no future introduction
No other meeting
As each day passes
I move closer and closer
To saying goodbye
And being forgotten

Feeling Alone

For those who feel left out
You are not alone.
For those who make excuses
Just to make themselves feel more accomplished
You are not alone.
For those who look in the mirror
Brush through their hair
Brown, black, blonde
Thick or thin
Wishing they were someone else
You are not alone.
For those who dream
Of walking across the sky
Sailing throughout space
Travelling as far away from the rest of civilization
To believe you are the only one
You are not alone.
For those who—
Who want to be better
Want to wake up each morning
Smell the air
Feel its breeze
Open your eyes
See the light
And understand
You are who you are
You are not alone.

For those who want to change things about themselves
You are better than you think you are
When you jump
Feet barely leaving the ground
Look again
You will see yourself amongst the clouds
Moisture absorbing into your skin
Rejuvenation
For those who feel as if they are alone
You are not alone.

Empty Room

As I sit here
Tears falling down my face
Trembling hands
With only these words keeping me still

Looking around this room
Full of thoughts and memories
Yet completely empty without you
Each moment passing slower than the last
Counting every second
Hoping you walk through that door

I want you here
I want to be there

Being apart no longer makes sense
Each day is another opportunity lost
To look into your eyes
Take you in
Implant your image
Record your voice
Playback your smile

Remembering becomes punishing
Straining my mind to find happiness
This room containing empty shelves filled with dreams and memories
Sliding off their slanted edges
No bookend can hold what I am losing

The carpeted floor may have soaked up what has fallen
But I will forever step on what I once remembered
Leaving a footprint I would rather forget

Steady

What Is Poetry?

Poetry is the means of expressing the reality that the heart fails to realize.

(Untitled)

They tell you to keep your head up
They say
It will get better
You have nothing to worry about
They have no idea what you are dealing with
Fourteen-hour work days
Long commutes in traffic
Which seems endless
You tell yourself:
"If I get out now I can probably walk home faster."
They have no idea
That after work
You are taking extra courses
Raising a family
Caring for a pet
Dealing with your constant depression and distress
Of failing
Of falling apart
Every night
You spend
Eyes fully opened
Constantly thinking of what is to come
Why you are wasting time sitting there
Instead of completing the next task
All night
Until the alarm sounds
And the horror of the day begins
They think
Your problems are easy to face
They think you will just get over them
They never ask the questions you want to hear

Are you okay?

Do you need help?

I am going to help you

I will listen to you

I am with you

Note to Self

I tell myself,
Everything will be okay
I tell myself,
Everything will be fine
I tell myself,
The mountain is not as steep as it seems
Even while I am sliding backwards down it

I tell myself,
To take another step forward
Keep going
Keep your head up
Keep moving

I tell myself,
You are happy
You are fulfilled
You are better than what you think you are

I tell myself,
There are good days and bad days
Most days there is no difference
As if I am riding the merry-go-round
Forever in a loop
Never in control of my next step

I tell myself,
Soak in the sadness
Absorb everything you are feeling like a sponge
So you can squeeze it all out before the next day begins

They Are

They are indescribable
They are mine
They are yours
They are together
They are here
They are there
They are them
They are free
They are more
They are simple
They are forever more
They are one

Changes

Tonight, we are going to change the world
Each step, one at a time
Finding the path through the road swirled
Reaching the top after its wondrous climb

Each movement is another near
To our greatest victory of all
Where every moment is clear
Watching, and waiting for your call

Finding more through these changes
All leading up to this
While, again, the world rearranges
Ending up wandering in an endless abyss
Forgetting how this came to be

New

I know I am not alone
But I feel that way
Everywhere I walk
Everywhere I stare
I am alone on a path
That can only lead to another lonely place
I do not know where this place is
I do not know when I will get there
If time is all it takes
I should stop here and wait
For one to take me away
From this closed state of mind
In order to free myself
With one by my side
All it takes is one
Only one
But that one needs to know
The path which I am headed down
Exposing a new world to explore
One with you
And you with me
For only then this feeling fades
During the next era of our days
Headed down this path unfazed
Shoulder to shoulder
Hand in hand
Together

Stuck behind a Curtain

As I stand off stage
Sweat dripping down my face
Tasting each drop as it crosses my lips
A thousand thoughts running through my mind
Am I okay?
Will I screw up?

I wonder what is on the other side
A sea of eyes
Ready to pass judgment
Pointing out every mistake
There is only doubt
And I begin to tremble

When I glance around me
Noticing the other performers
Concentration flowing through
Each glimpse of their surroundings
Only time will tell
If they are truly ready

I try to regain focus
Thick clouds block my vision
Forcing me to pace
Anticipating the draw of the curtain
Only to feel time slow
Prolonging
                        My
                                        Anxiety
I hear the director in the background:
"We begin in 5, 4, 3..."
All I can do is breathe
(Inhale ... Exhale ...)
Stepping onto the stage
Ready as the curtain begins to rise

Appreciation

Appreciation
No need to say less
Everything in your life
Happens because you make it so

Make it all your own
Remember how you got there
Remember the people along the way
You may not see it now
But they were everything to you

Show righteousness in victory
And honour in defeat
Lest forget the details
They made all the difference

As the days pass by
You may be keeping up
Or get lost in the shuffle

Just don't forget
Never forget
All that you have
Appreciate

Move Forward

Light is what shines around you
Growing more as time goes on
Becoming the one I find true
And light my way until dawn

People see me and laugh
I feel as if I should hide
Happiness drops like a declining graph
Though in my sorrow, you are the one I find

Help me move forward through life
Never letting me back down
Moving through like a sharp knife
Makes me believe I'm a golden crown

I go on throughout my day
As you go on as well
My mind is going grey
Forever wondering if you can tell

Forging something new being together
Always as one forever

Pursuit of Perfection

You know I am not a poet
But when I feel the urge
Before I write
Veins begin to pulse
Heart beating to the rhythm of a drum
Which can only be heard
Within the confines of my bedroom
Every image I ever had
Covered
Underneath its dark blue paint
With no poster placed over them
But words which constantly occupy my mind
Chapter by Chapter
Page by Page
Every word continuing to another
Endlessly

Then I stop breathing
Air is still
Body is calm
Inhale
Then I begin

I want to write the perfect poem
But I know I can't
Every thought formed in my mind
The flashes of words
Continuation of phrases
Formulating around my brain
Surging more words and phrases
That hit the page in disorder
Leaving me trapped underneath my pen

I want to write the perfect words
But I know I can't
It is like when I first rode my bike
Which only had one speed
Along the dusty brown country road
Because there was no rush
No need to move any faster
With the seat just a little higher than it should be
High enough that when I sat
I could barely reach the pedals
Accelerating faster
Then slowing down
Tilting
Crashing onto the pavement
Front wheel bending sideways
Suddenly in need of repair

I want to write the perfect poem
But I know I can't
I know I can dream of one
Every piece of imagination
Seen through the telescope outside my window
Looking out into the sunset
Sunlight reflecting off the land
The water revealing the stars
Sparkling amongst each other
Becoming the words which
Form onto my paper

When I am finished
I read it over
Then sink into my seat
Slowly slipping
Closer to hitting the floor
Wondering what went wrong.
Why is it not perfect?
Why can't I write a perfect poem?
The only problem with that thought
Is not about writing a perfect poem
Because there is no such thing as one
And what I have written
In that moment
Is the closest to perfect as it will ever be

Resilience

Until I Write

I may not write something every day
I may not write something every week
I may not write something every month
But when I do write
It keeps me moving forward
Until I write again

Rise

First,
I want you to stand
Not only through your posture
But through every fibre of your being
I want your presence known

Second,
Take your hands
Place them together
And pray that each step you take
Brings you closer to your goal
Take your hands and fight

Third,
Believe

Fourth,
Start being true to yourself
You will get nowhere
If you can't find your own reflection

Fifth,
Take everything in
Every ounce of knowledge
Every taste of friendship
Every drop of love
Allowing you to fully be alive
Rise
Not just for those who believe in you
But for yourself
Rise
Because you need to

Vase

So
You want to know how to break me
How to shake me and bend me
How to shatter me and scatter me

It is easy
First start with dust
Put enough pressure on it
Turn each grain into sand.
Then take a flame
Melt it down and mould it
Into a vase
Put any decoration you want on it
Make it as big or as small as you please
But don't get used to it

Fill the vase with water
Overflow it with your thoughts
Let it fall over the sides
Covering each inch of the design
Until all you see is yourself
Upon the reflection

Take a flower
Whichever you prefer
A lily for peace
Sunflower for light
Gardenia for every scent that is right
Place it into your creation
Having it absorb your mind
Blossoming from your emotions
Letting its fragrance fill the air
Taking the place of pain
So it doesn't seem as bad
As it may initially feel

Find a place for this vase
A safe place
A place where
Even if it falls
It won't break
Maybe in your bedroom
Just to keep it close
While you are dreaming
And when you wake
It is the first image you see
Just to keep you smiling
For a little while longer

Keep it close and near
Just as you do with your feelings
Don't let it drift too far away
You may lose yourself
Only when you are ready
You can let the vase go
Even if that means
Climbing to the highest point you can
Holding the vase outstretched
Over the edge
Emotionless
You got what you needed from it
And now you can let it go

Watch
Listen
As the vase screams and falls
The inevitable fate which you gave it
Crashing onto the ground
Only dust remains
Unable to be reassembled
Left to drift along
Lost among the rest of the Earth
While you carry onward

And when you understand this feeling
A vase for you shall be made

I Have and I Will

I have groomed myself to be stern
Noble and genuine
I have learned
To fear the things I have become comfortable with
In order to fully understand the limits of my sanity
I have grown
To outlast hate and gather love
To gain a new perspective on life
I will live
And pursue greatness
For today
Will generate the happiness
I will feel tomorrow

Catch of the Day

You have kept me so close
For so long
Fishing me along
With the end of your line
Only until I bite
You pull me in

Hoist me out of the water
Set me on land
Watching as I gasp for air
Within your clutches
You stare as I pulse
Faster and faster I breathe
Trying to catch the last bit of air
Before you plunge me back in
Only to try and catch me again

I am just a game
No more
No less
A ploy to give you satisfaction
For those short moments of glory

Just a cheap laugh
A simple joke only you understand
Since you are the only audience member
In a stadium built for us

While I stand upon the stage
You sit
Front row centre
Poised to cheer for more
Ready
Popcorn in hand
Drink in its holder
Half-finished from your anticipation
Of the show ahead

Though when I walk away
You can't move
So used to those caught by you
To see the other side
How the prey feels
Put in a position
Where laughter is all we know
Mocking is how we grow

We don't need any more of you
Try as you may
Catch as many more as you please
But we will learn
And soon
You won't be laughing so hard

Driving on a Road I Continue to Build

Trying to find a new way to express myself
My feelings
And my soul
Then the wall begins to form in front of me
Challenging me to do the impossible
Win a race against myself

I've been losing the race so far
But catching up along the way
A few more feet and as I look down the path
A sight only making me fall farther behind

This World

It is something that happens every so often
Self-doubt forming inside me
Building like a virus
Small at first
Then suddenly
Taking me over
Replacing every ounce of courage I have ever built up
Disappearing
Leaving me in this pit
With no possible way of escaping
As I see the sun cross over
The darkness creeps upon me
It overtakes me
Bringing me into the world
That I hope to never see again
You see
This world scares me more than
Falling out of a plane without a parachute
Hitting the ground to only wake up again
This world is like being choked
By an invisible man
The only reason to gasp for air
Is to see your own hand around your neck
This world
Takes your soul and tears away at it
As if you're in a shredder
Slowly losing yourself
With your screams heard by no one
I need to be saved from this world
Dying from the inside
Leaving the body empty in the end
This is not how I saw myself
I need to be saved because I know
That someone will be waiting for me
On the other side
To keep me close

Never let me go
Even if they don't understand
As long as they try
That is all I ask for

Forget

Forget today
Forget tomorrow
Forget,
The moment I can never take back
Clutching the very thing I could never let go

You

Forget,
Doubting all of my actions
Taking an extra second to question a decision
I was never going to make in the first place

Forget,
Wanting something better for myself
This is it
This is all
This is everything

Forget,
Thinking it is over
I am still here
I will keep going
I will keep going

About the Author

Although he did not pursue a degree in literature, Cosimo explored and expanded his poetry in his early twenties. Moving away for university allowed him to experience a whole other world compared to the one he grew up in. This led to many encounters with love, sadness, depression and anger. The only outlet that had an effect on his mental health was his poetry. Writing allowed him to feel and process his emotions through art.

Putting pen to paper was the last thing on his mind as he grew up in the small town of Bolton, Ontario, Canada. Cosimo spent most of his time outside or participating in sports. Growing up in Canada allowed him to appreciate the value of community, where he recognized the impact one person can have on others within a small town.

His love for poetry emerged from one of his high school teachers, Mr. Adriano, when he challenged Cosimo about what writing can be. Once graduating high school Cosimo completed his bachelor's degree in archaeology at Sir Wilfrid Laurier University. He then spent seven years working in the world of archaeology alongside First Nations communities in Southern Ontario.

Cosimo is currently an elementary school teacher hoping to share his love of history and poetry with his students. He is married and has recently become a father.

www.ingramcontent.com/pod-product-compliance
Lightning Source LLC
Chambersburg PA
CBHW030512130626
46549CB00007B/2958